What to *Say*

52 Positive Ways to Show Christian Sympathy to Those Who Grieve

Carol Fredericks Ebeling

This book is dedicated to

• Hundreds of individuals who opened their homes to me during my years as hospice director. Some taught me how to ask for help, while others were masters in stepping forward with a unique gift of caring.

• Children, teens, and adults in grief support groups who related words and deeds that comforted them and those that did not.

• My husband, Dave, for sharing with me his experience of being a college student whose father died and for his unending support of me in writing this book.

1 2 3 4 5 6 7 8 9 10   11 10 09 08 07 06 05 04 03 02

Contents

Introduction

As a Christian caregiver, you want to respond to people experiencing loss. You want to do the right and helpful thing. You want to let those who are grieving know you care without being a burden to them.

Jesus certainly did this in His ministry. When Lazarus died, Jesus comforted his sister Martha, saying, "Your brother will rise again" (John 11:23). These are words of great consolation to all who believe in the one true God and hope for the resurrection of the dead. Then, to the astonishment of everyone, Jesus actually raised Lazarus from the dead (John 11:43–44). By this miracle He showed Himself to be the Son of God who would soon lay down His life for our sins on the cross and take His life back again in the resurrection. Through faith in Him we have the free gift of eternal life. By the Sacrament of Holy Baptism, we are filled with His Spirit. The Holy Spirit inspires us and enables us to do good works, such as comforting those who mourn (Isaiah 61:2).

When a terminal illness is diagnosed, when a death occurs, or when you feel the need to keep in touch with a grieving person after a death, it is normal to think or even say out loud, "But, I don't know what to say! I don't know what to do!"

Sometimes the situation is so sad that you choose to say or do nothing, rather than risk saying or doing the wrong thing. Sometimes you are literally at a loss for words and choose to stay away rather than risk embarrassing yourself. There is not a universally "correct" thing to say or do in all situations. People are unique individuals, and, therefore, each person will respond in unique ways.

But there are words you can **say** that are usually appropriate.

There are things you can **do** that are usually helpful.

However you choose to show sympathy—that you know someone is experiencing a loss and that you care—is almost always better than saying and doing nothing. Your response, whether verbal, written, or visual, provides an indication that you care about other people. Your behavior is a practical witness to your love of Christ. For example, have you ever noticed how often Jesus touched people? When Peter's mother-in-law was sick, Jesus "went to her, took her hand and helped her up" (Mark 1:31). A poor leper came to Jesus and begged for healing. "Filled with compassion, Jesus reached out His hand and touched the man" (Mark 1:41). Of course the divine Son of God performed miraculous healings for these people and many others. But the fact of His touching people shows His manly compassion.

In Paul's letter to his Christian friends in Rome, he listed short, specific words of advice for Christians to show love to others because of Christ's sacrifice for us.

> Love must be sincere.
> Hate what is evil;
> > cling to what is good.
> Be devoted to one another in
> > brotherly love.
> Honor one another above yourselves.
> Never be lacking in zeal,
> > but keep your spiritual fervor,
> > serving the Lord.
> Be joyful in hope,
> > patient in affliction,
> > faithful in prayer.
> Share with God's people who are in need.
> Practice hospitality.
> Bless those who persecute you;
> > bless and do not curse.
> Rejoice with those who rejoice;
> > mourn with those who mourn.
>
> Romans 12:9–15

The good works listed here are preceded by 11 chapters of solid doctrinal theology in which Christ's atoning work on the cross, His glorious resurrection, and the resulting justification by grace through faith are described in matchless detail. As in the letter, so in our lives, all we do is backed up by all we believe.

Your interest in other people, your ability to listen, your words of comfort, your intentional reaching out, your continuing communications, your remembering what others forget—all these enable grieving persons to mourn. You literally "mourn with those who mourn" and thereby uphold one another in times of grief.

There are numerous books and pamphlets already on bookstore shelves and pamphlet racks that accurately remind us what *not* to say and do. Those are important to read and heed. This book, in contrast, approaches the grieving situation from a positive viewpoint. Here you will find a collection of specific words to say and actions to take to show someone you care. Many of these are commonsense suggestions; many are specifically Christian. But all flow from a heart of faith that is shaped by the love of God in Christ. Note also that all of these situations and suggestions apply equally to men and women.

Grieving can happen over a long period of time: (1) during a terminal illness, (2) at the time of a death, (3) following trauma, when there is no closure, but the aftermath of the trauma remains permanently, and/or (4) in the months and years following a death. I have observed people of all ages grasping for the right words to say or the right thing to do whenever and wherever there is grief.

All the ideas in this collection come from personal experience. I have tried them, heard about them from those who were mourning, observed them, or recommended them in some form as a private counselor or the director of a hospice program. I've spent countless hours at the bedside of terminal patients. I've talked late into the night with family members trying to come to grips with a terminal illness, a sudden death, or adjustments to drastically different life after a death. I've held the hands of dozens of people as they breathed their last breath. I've met grieving families at the funeral home door when they arrive to make arrangements for services. I've maintained contact with grieving people on a systematic basis for at least 13 months after each death. That's all part of the hospice approach to caring for terminally ill persons and their families.

Even though I have had those experiences—or perhaps, because of it—I am still in awe of life and death. As a Christian woman, I marvel at God's gift of life. I have been blessed to experience two full-term pregnancies. And I also know the sadness of miscarriage. While God was creating and growing those babies, my body, heart, soul, and mind were also changing in preparation for giving birth. I was one of the many women who have had complications, including hospitalization, during this process. Other women breeze through the process hardly noticing more than the change in their dress size.

At both ends of the life cycle there are vast changes. At both times the event happening to the key person affects many others as well. At both times there are opportunities to give our Christian witness through word and deed. God the Holy Spirit can and will give you grace to speak to others about the hope that is in you through Christ. Life begins for each of us as infants who, unquestionably, must depend on others for every form of care. Life ends for many of us with needs that once again exceed our ability to be independent. God sustains each of us in His own time, giving life and calling His children home to heaven. This is nothing less than awesome.

PART 1

Bereavement, Grief, and Mourning

The airport connection was going to be tight. I was flying from Indianapolis to Buffalo to speak at a conference. The airline schedule allowed 45 minutes to make a connection at Detroit. The first leg was running late, so I'd have to hustle to learn where the connecting gate was located and to get there in time to complete my trip. With just a few minutes to spare, I was the last one to board the flight to Buffalo.

I slipped into my seat, relieved that I did not have to deal with a missed flight. I was readjusting my carry-on bag when I noticed the zipper was open. A quick glance, then frantic rummaging, and I realized my appointment book was not in the bag.

— The process of *bereavement* had begun.

I lost something. As soon as I discovered the loss, my

entire being changed. What had been relief turned to disbelief, frustration, anger, uncertainty, self-doubt, and deep concern about what I would do next. I was frozen in time and space. I tried to recall when I had last seen the appointment book, when I last looked in my carry-on bag, what I was doing that made me fail to zip it shut as I got off the last plane. At this point, there was no one on the plane, no member of my family, no one at the conference I was soon to address, who knew anything about my loss. It was just me—in seat 22B—in this state of grief.

— I was *grieving*.

Inside me, and me alone, my physical, mental, and emotional systems were in turmoil. The fact that I lost something is bereavement; the lonely, individual feeling of that loss is grief. As you read about my plight, you probably recalled times when you have had similar losses. That is empathy, and it can be an extremely helpful emotion to mobilize you to say or do something to help. It is not, however, knowledge of how I was grieving that day.

The flight from Detroit to Buffalo is less than an hour. I intended to spend my time reviewing presentation notes and maybe catching a brief nap. Instead, I was totally consumed with the loss of my appointment book. I was not interested in the pretzels and drink offered by the flight attendant. I couldn't take a short nap. I couldn't focus on reviewing my agenda. The passenger seated next to me must have sensed something was wrong, perhaps because of the numerous times I had searched my carry-on bag, the pockets of my coat, and the space around my seat. "Are you okay?" she asked inquisitively. "Oh, I just lost my calendar somewhere on this trip," I shrugged.

— Now I am *mourning*.

I've gone public with my grief. Someone else, besides me, knows about my loss. With each telling, I'll feel a bit closer to finding a way to deal with my loss. Eventually I will tell others and each will react differently, some with empathetic concern, others with casual indifference, and almost all with a story of their own about a time when they lost something. But the fact that others now know about my loss has taken me into the stage called "mourning."

As it was with the appointment book incident, so it is with any loss, especially with death. It is natural. It is necessary. Review these three terms and their definitions again:

You lose something.

This is *bereavement*: the act of being bereft or cut off from something.

You react to it internally.

This is *grief*: your personal, physical, emotional, and mental reaction to the loss.

If you are fortunate, people let you share your grief publicly.

This is *mourning*: the public sharing and display of grief. Without mourning, grief often leads to relational and other personal problems.

In many cases we, as caring Christians, are not bereft (someone close to us did not die) and we are not grieving (feelings of personal loss.) But we are a part of the mourning process—an important part. We become the "public" in the definition of mourning, "grief made public."

The Cumulative Effect of Losses

These three—bereavement, grief, and mourning—are cyclical and cumulative. The process repeats itself over and over with another diagnosis, another procedure, another accident, another death, another loss.

By the time a person dies, the family may have experienced all three of these emotions numerous times. For example:

Bereavement: Dad is diagnosed with cancer. You've *lost the good health* of a family member.

Grief: Your mind spins with how life will be different as you learn to cope with this illness.

Mourning: You tell selected family members about Dad's diagnosis, and you plan for the treatments ahead. You cry together.

Months later, Dad seems to be stable, even doing well. Then . . .

Bereavement: Dad complains of a major pain in his abdomen. You've *lost hope* for a complete recovery.

Grief: Your mind and heart suspect that the cancer has spread. You get more test results, and the fear is confirmed.

Mourning: You gather the family and tell them about the new diagnosis. Now that the cancer has spread, chances of a cure are diminished.

Dad's health levels off for a while, then . . .

Bereavement: Dad's energy is totally spent. He no longer leaves the house or even participates in conversation. You've *lost lifestyle and companionship.*

Grief: You envision the lifestyle change that will tie you to the house and cut you off from normal social interactions. You actually rehearse in your mind the time Dad will die.

Mourning: You tell your pastor that you are frightened, that it takes all your energy to care for your dad and your own family.

In each of these three scenarios, Dad is still alive. Yet, the loved ones are experiencing bereavement, grief, and mourning with each stage in the illness. You think you are well-prepared for the inevitable death. When Dad does actually die, the family is surprised by the intensity of their pain as they go through the cycle once again.

A Personal Case Study

My own parents died 10 days apart in spring of 1993.

For the previous several years, the rapid progression of their aging process and chronic illnesses brought me to the realization that Mom and Dad were nearing the end of their lives. Many times we had had trips to the hospital that set the bereavement process in motion. They lost vigor, interest in former hobbies, and ability to keep straight all the events and people in their daily lives. There were cancers, strokes, bouts with pneumonia, broken hips. Many times we were bereft over the new loss, grieved it, mourned it together, adjusted to it, and went on living.

Then one Thursday, while I was 250 miles from home attending a national church meeting, a phone call alerted me to Mom's closeness to death. Part of me was hurled into denial; she had always regained strength following every previous crisis. The other part of me "knew what I knew"; this time was different. God really was ready to take her to her heavenly home.

I was an experienced hospice director. I knew exactly what to do, whom to call, how to talk with Dad. I knew it was wise and helpful to offer Dad one last opportunity to rest beside Mom in her hospital bed, rather than have only memories of recent times separated by wheelchairs and separate beds. The intellectual side of me was well-prepared and organized. The personal, emotional side was crumbling under the burden. God gave us five long days to pray and sing Mom's favorite hymns for her; to support Dad in his difficult time of understanding what was happening; to carefully reassure her that we would care for

Dad and for each other; and to tell her of our love. We "gave her permission to die," and we prepared him—and us—for a final good-bye.

For years I had encouraged hospice volunteers to offer house-sitting service to grieving families because of the disarming statistics that indicate thieves prey on households of survivors around the time of a visitation and funeral. This proved to be another new experience for me when someone attempted to break into our home at 5:30 A.M. Our loud security alarm interrupted the theft, and the police arrived in minutes. Yet now I had to grieve also the loss of my safety.

Ten days later, while at work, my morning was interrupted by a phone call from the nursing home telling me that Dad was being "difficult." He had refused his medications and his breakfast and had asked to go to the hospital. The attending nurse didn't believe he was ill. The bereavement process began again. It took several calls before I persuaded the staff to send Dad to the hospital where I was working, whether they felt it was warranted or not. Since he had just buried Mom, and he felt sick enough to ask for help, he needed to know staff would care for him. It wasn't long before the emergency room doctor paged me to say that Dad had nearly died en route to the hospital. His congestive heart and lung problems were critical. The "bereavement/grief/mourning" wheel was spinning faster. There wasn't time to process what was happening.

17

People needed to be called. My husband, son, and son-in-law were all out of town on business trips. My daughter was teaching school and would need to have her classroom covered. Other out-of-town relatives had barely returned home to their routines since the last funeral trip. God gave Dad about eight hours in which to hear my daughter and me tell him of our love and to convey loving messages from other key family members as we reached them by phone. Those eight hours were a special gift also to prepare us for what was about to happen. Did having that time soften the shock of watching him die? Not at all. There is no way to anticipate exactly what you will feel when death actually occurs, even with illness, or aging, or both, leading the way. The bereavement/grieving/mourning process began anew at 6 P.M. when the cardiologist pronounced Dad dead.

Grief and Mourning without Bereavement

I scan the obituary column of my local paper. My eyes are drawn to the news report that a local 12-year-old boy died at Children's Hospital. I don't know the family, but I read the details anyway, because it was a child who died. "He was preceded in death," details the obituary, "by two sisters. All three have died from metachromatic leukodystrophy, a genetic disease."

A family is bereft. It is to be without this child as well as his two sisters. I am not bereft. I was not cut off from someone I love. I am not experiencing bereavement.

But I grieve. My immediate thought is that of a cousin who lost two children to a genetic disease. I internalize the bereavement notice of a child in the community and transfer it to a personal experience. My husband did not think of the cousin who is still in the early phases of adjusting to a similar double loss. Upon reading the same obituary, he reflected that our own daughter's family includes two girls and a boy, and he remarked how devastating it would be to lose all three in an almost predictable set of uncontrollable circumstances. My husband grieved, too, but differently from me.

And we mourn. As soon as we expressed to each other what impact that local obituary had on our minds and hearts, we entered into the more healing experience of mourning. Now our grief was made public, if only to each other. We empathize with each other, sharing specific thoughts that sadden us. We may not grieve or mourn very long, but all the emotions find their way through our hearts and minds. And when conversation ends, we know that our grief is likely to resurface later. Still, as Christians we grieve, but not like those "who have no hope" (1 Thessalonians 4:13). Many who exist without Christ are "held in slavery by their fear of death" (Hebrews 2:15). When thrown into grief by the experience of death, they don't know what to think or do. We Christians have the sure hope of the resurrection to comfort us and can say with confidence, "Where, O death, is your victory?" (1 Corinthians 15:55). We who have faith have unseen resources to draw on when we suffer, and we have an extra measure of hope to share with those who grieve but do not yet believe.

Grief Revisited

Grief is revisited many times throughout our lives. The obituary of the child we did not know quickly brought to mind other deaths. Over 30 years ago our newborn infant daughter hovered between life and death for her first five months. She survived, but a year later I suffered an early miscarriage. A close friend delivered a son about the time our daughter was gaining strength; he became ill and lived less than a year. Another dear friend gave birth to twins; only one infant survived the first week. A niece carried her son to full-term, but he strangled on his umbilical cord as she drove from the doctor's office to the hospital delivery room. A cousin lost both of his primary-school-age sons within two years to a rare genetic disease.

As we learn of someone's death, our hearts are touched again by the past. If we deny this, or ignore its importance, the silent pain is likely to affect other areas of our lives. Tempers may flare, job performance declines, health suffers. This is an important time to talk with a friend, family member, or pastor about the grief that is being recalled. When we make our personal feelings public, mourn them, we limit their negative impact on our lives.

Children must be helped to review the deaths of loved ones as they progress through the various developmental stages of life. If a grandfather dies when a child is preschool age, there will be questions and gaps of understanding that must be addressed regularly as the child matures. He may be saddened and feel isolated from members of the family who had more contact with Grandpa. He may have lingering questions about the death and funeral details that he cannot recall. With many future deaths, the past will loom larger. And it may be happening in such a confused state that he doesn't know what questions to ask.

Our oldest grandchild, Hannah, celebrated her first birthday during the 10 days that separated Mom's and Dad's deaths. Hannah's memories of the two of them are certainly limited to family stories. Rachel, now seven, is 20 months younger than Hannah. A few days ago while Rachel was alone with me, she said, "Hannah was really, really lucky because she got to know Great-Grandma and Great-Grandpa before they died. And just think, if God had waited only one more month to take them, Mom could have told them she was pregnant with me. Do you think that would have made them die happier?" This is at least the third time Rachel has mentioned she feels left out by not knowing the great-grandparents her sister knew. Each time her curiosity includes a slightly more mature perspective. We look at their pictures, tell a story or two, and talk about their personal traits, especially the ones that seem to have been passed down to Rachel. And my daughter also has these family history sessions, not only regarding her two grandparents, but her husband's family as well.

What to Expect in Grief

In some respects, grief is like an onion. A full ripe onion is quite large, but as the layers are peeled away one by one, the onion gets smaller and smaller. Our grief, too, must be peeled away one layer at a time. Only that way can we process all the bitter pain and reduce it to a size that we can live with for the rest of our lives.

Expect Shock and Protest

"How can this be? Surely things aren't as bad as they seem." Grief feelings are often hidden or masked by the shock of the news, which can delay the grieving process. Don't attempt to jar someone out of this reaction. It is God's emotional shock absorber for us until He equips us with greater strength to handle the pain. The funeral process is a very important part of that preparation. As tiring as visitation hours can be, the support of others at this time is of great value.

Expect Suffering and Despair

"Things couldn't be worse. How can I go on?"

This phase often takes four to six months to hit. At that time, most previously supportive individuals have gone back to their routines. Not understanding how long grief feelings may remain masked, many people have interpreted the mourner's behavior as being "over it." This is precisely the time period when the "everydayness" of living without the deceased has sunk in with a jarring thud. Mark your calendar to remind you to call, visit, or send a note particularly about six months after the death.

Expect Reconciliation and Reorganization

"Who am I now?" Death takes from us so much more than a parent, confidant, lover, or dear child. We lose our identity, as well as the loved one, when death occurs.

— If an adult loses a parent, he loses his *past*. When the second parent dies, he may feel like a virtual orphan. No one else has ever known certain things or experienced his growing up in the same way. There is no one else to call when a memory of childhood is triggered. There may be no one else to ask about details of family history.

— If an adult loses a spouse, she loses her *present*. Whatever their relationship was, from the moment of their engagement, she saw herself in a unique way through the eyes of her husband.

— If an adult loses a child, he loses his *future*. Whenever pregnancy is medically confirmed, parents and grandparents redesign their entire future based on the addition of one more child. If that child dies, even before birth, there is a lifetime of lost plans, unfulfilled dreams, empty arms.

Time does not heal grief, but over time grief takes on new characteristics. There are moments that feel like eternity, and, eventually, there are hours that slip by with surprising calmness. Many people grieve anew when they fear that they may be losing the sound of their loved one's voice. So, as people who want to be helpful during these difficult months, how do we recognize any signs of reorganizing their lives?

Children grieve differently from adults, processing all information in accord with their present developmental level. They have four tasks of grief.

1. *Understanding.* They need enough accurate information to understand the circumstances. It is tempting to think we are protecting them by not sharing details, but children will always fill in gaps in information. Their imagination is at least as graphic and frightening as reality, and it is usually worse.

2. *Grieving.* Here, too, adults often wish to protect them. Adults will run to the bathroom to cry alone, rather than cry in front of a child. The child learns that tears are not part of the adult experience. As he feels his own sadness, he feels childish and inferior. He then shuts out his own grief to protect the adults. I have counseled with many adults who still have unresolved grief from childhood and find it difficult to take emotional risks.

3. *Commemorating.* Scrapbooks, bulletin boards, tape

recordings, and drawing pictures help children to commemorate the life of the deceased. It is important to keep family pictures on display, talk about the loved one on special occasions, and keep the memories alive. This also teaches children that we honor all life that God has created, rather than quickly forgetting our ancestors and friends when death occurs.

4. *Moving on*. Children have shorter attention spans than adults. This often is a source of tension between them. Adults stay with their feelings for a long time, and it appears to them that children are not showing proper respect. Children will ask questions, deal with the answers, and turn to play or work on something unrelated. Later, however, the same questions and issues will resurface. One five-year-old cried when he saw his father in the casket, but before leaving the funeral home, he asked his mother, "Will Daddy be back from heaven for my ballgame on Friday?"

How Do We Recognize Someone Is Reorganizing His Life in a Healthy Way?

There are four indicators that a person is making progress adapting to the loss of his loved one and reorganizing life in a healthy way.

1. She has the ability to *use the hard words*. Rather than euphemisms like "He's *gone*," the words spoken are, "He *died*."

2. He has the ability to *talk about the loss without being overwhelmed by tears.* That doesn't mean there are no tears, just that they no longer seem to control life.

3. She can *feel good about feeling good.* When she hears a funny comment, she allows herself to smile or even laugh without feeling guilty.

4. He *can risk change.* There is enough renewal of energy and well-being that he can do something different from the way he has been doing it since the death. Perhaps he begins to read cookbooks and prepare simple meals, rather than depending on fast-food restaurants and donations from friends. Still, friends and family are so important to the grieving person. Often we don't know what to say or do to help them. Here follow a year's worth of practical suggestions—things you can say and do as motivated by the love of Christ, who "went around doing good" (Acts 10:38).

~

PART 2

52 Positive Ways to Show Christian Sympathy to Those Who Grieve

This list of 52 ideas covers many areas of life—and death—but it is not intended to be exhaustive. Read through the ideas to find one that might work for you in a given situation. Modify any suggestion to better fit your personal need. Even use the margins to note the date you used an idea and the person who benefited from your care. Keep it handy and refer to it when you have the need. Add your own ideas in the margins to remember for future occasions.

ᗆ 1

Make Contact as Soon as Possible

Teachers call it the "teachable moment." In hospice work, we might call it the "caring moment." It's that time, soon after the death, when you make contact with a grieving person.

What you want to convey to a grieving friend, relative, or acquaintance is that the person's grief is very unique. You recognize that the death may be having a devastating effect. You can't and you won't pretend to know the exact feeling that is numbing the person.

Do: Go to the residence or the funeral home. This is a good time for a solid handshake, a gentle hug, or an appropriate touch on the shoulder or arm.

Say: "I am so sorry to hear of your _____'s death"; or "I extend to you my Christian condolences"; or "I'm sorry for your loss"; or "I'm praying that God will give you peace and comfort."

Even if you think you have had much the same loss experience as the person grieving, you haven't. Each of us brings different personal strengths, weaknesses, and previous experiences to bear on the grief event. No two people grieve alike, so you want to respect the differences.

〜 2

Make Reference to Personal Characteristics

When you're speaking to a survivor you know, but you didn't know the person who died, look for the characteristics in the survivor that may have been passed down from the deceased. This is especially useful when the parent of a friend or colleague has died.

Do: Talk to the person as soon as possible. You might go to the funeral home or simply wait until the person returns to work after the funeral.

Say: "I didn't know your mother (father, grandmother, etc.), but I do know you. I've always observed you as really compassionate with people who are hurting. Could it be that your mom was the same way? What can you tell me about her?"

You pick the characteristic. It might be the love of a sport, a shared hobby, or a commitment to a particular cause. Whatever it is, this lead comment provides an opening for the grieving person to respond. You may get a simple, "Thank you." You may spark a thought that will bring a smile and a good memory. Even if the mother was not the compassionate type, you did acknowledge a strength of your friend to the grieving person, and no harm was done.

3

"I'll Never Forget"

Use this sentence stem when you have had an experience with the deceased that is likely unknown to the survivor to whom you are speaking. It shows that you have a positive memory and that the thought of the situation you describe will not go away, even though the person has died.

For example, I remember speaking to the grieving adult daughter (whom I didn't know) about her deceased father (who was a member of my congregation): "I'll never forget," I began when I met her, "when my daughter was a baby and we were still in our small, original sanctuary. Your dad was an usher. One Sunday my husband was serving Communion as an elder, and I had our two small children in the back pew. Our infant daughter fell asleep. Your father reached over gently and offered to hold her while I walked to the Communion rail with my toddler. That began a frequent routine with John that I'll always fondly remember."

Do: Reflect on the life of the person deceased and capture a memory unique to the two of you. Then intentionally look for the opportunity to tell the story to a survivor.

Say: "Your _____ (sister-in-law, dad, grandmother, etc.) had a real zeal for _____. I remember the time _____.

What do you remember? Tell the story to someone who will value hearing it.

⌒ 4

Shine Shoes

When a death takes place, usually a funeral is only a day or two away. The family has so many things to consider regarding the funeral arrangements that they likely will have little time or energy to consider the smaller details of personal grooming. You can offer to take on the modern equivalent of the foot washing modeled by Jesus with His disciples. Instead of foot washing, make it shoe shining.

Do: Pack up your own shoeshine supplies (several colors of polish, a shoeshine brush, and an old soft cloth) and simply show up at the door of the grieving family.

Say: "I'm so sorry for your loss. I came by to offer help in a small way. If you would get the family's shoes together, I'll shine them so you will feel well-dressed at the funeral."

The grieving person may not accept the offer. If accepted, however, you'll have a few minutes to talk while you do the shoe shining. If your offer is declined, you have made an offer that will be remembered. Either way, when their eyes are downcast during the hours they stand beside the casket, they will remember your loving gesture. They will know that you are someone to whom they can go when they need a friend. You'll do anything.

5

Draw Pictures to Share Memories

One way to express grief is to illustrate it. Children often will not say anything and may not be able to express their feelings in words. Given a piece of paper and some writing or drawing tools, they can create pictures that convey volumes to the survivors.

Do: Invite children to write notes or draw pictures to share their memories with the grieving family. If you are in a position to guide the experience with a group of children, give each child an identical-sized piece of paper. Help the children remember some things about their teacher or classmate (or loved one) so they have several starter thoughts. Then allow enough time for the children to reflect, draw, color, and compose their thoughts. Have extra sheets available for children who want to start over or who want to add pages.

Display these memories awhile. It may be possible to make a display at the funeral home. Or they might be posted on a school or church bulletin board. At some point, within about 30 days, bind the sheets together in a three-ring binder or some other means and present the book of memories to the family.

Say: "Each of the children in our class drew a picture or composed a note to express their love for _____ _____. It was very important to each of them to tell you how much _____ meant to them. On their behalf, I am honored to present this scrapbook to you. We hope it will remain a reminder of how much we all care about you."

The process of preparing notes or pictures is a useful tool for the children who are grieving. Each memory displayed helps them deal with their grief personally and corporately within the group. Other people viewing the display will be given an opportunity to express their memories as well. The gift will be a treasure that the family will always cherish. One of the hardest factors of grief is thinking that other people may not care that your loved one has died. This gift demonstrates how large an impact this person's life has made on friends and peers.

ᔐ 6

Design and Make a Memorial Quilt

It is not unusual for churches to have a group of women who gather occasionally or regularly to quilt. Whether done as a group or an individual, the design and creation of a unique memorial quilt provides the opportunity for numerous people to share memories with the grieving family.

Do: Each square in the quilt could be a unique design reflecting a particular memory. Another approach is to make the quilt from a variety of designs around a theme. For instance, if the deceased person was an avid gardener, each square could be a different floral design.

When the quilt is complete, invite the survivors to a quilt dedication in memory of the deceased. Make it a party, a celebration, of the person's life. Hang the quilt in a public place for a while and post a written description of the meaning of the designs.

Say: "We dedicate this quilt to the memory of _____. For many years, she beautified her yard and the church property with colorful flowers. This quilt is presented to you, the family, as a lasting tribute to her and as a reminder to all who see it that she not only raised beautiful flowers, but also was a beautiful person."

On a national level, publicity has been given to the AIDS "Quilts Across America." These are meaningful to both the survivors and those who do the quilting.

∽ 7

Plant a Tree

Almost every property can use another tree or shrub. One way to honor the memory of someone is to plant a tree in a deceased person's memory. This is usually done weeks or even months after the death, usually at the appropriate planting time for the climate. Before purchasing the tree, check with the owners or managers of the property on which the tree is to be planted. There may be a landscape plan that requires a certain type of tree in a specific area. As part of your gift, establish a system to ensure that the tree is planted properly, nurtured during the first year, and intentionally maintained after that.

Create or have engraved some kind of plaque that states that this tree is planted in memory of a particular person. The plaque should be installed near the tree outside or framed and mounted inside a church or school building near a window that overlooks the area of the tree.

Do: Arrange a formal tree-planting ceremony. Invite the survivors to attend. Include numerous people to dig a shovel of soil where the tree will be planted. Have a short program dedicating the tree.

Say: Use words of comfort for the survivors and words of dedication of the tree. Focus on life and the fact that this live tree will always remind those who see it of the life of the loved one. "Today we plant this tree in memory of _____. It will be a reminder to those of us who pass by here of _____'s life and her joy when she was outside. As the seasons come and go, the tree, too, will change. We'll watch the budding, the blooming, and the preparation for winter."

ᔢ 8

House-sit during Visitation and Funeral Hours

As much as we would rather think this would not be necessary, there are evil people in this world who prey upon grieving families. They read obituaries to find out the time of the visitation at a funeral home or the funeral itself. There are plenty of public records and Internet sites that allow the evil people to find addresses of the deceased and the relatives. They see this as a most opportune time to break into homes and vehicles and steal whatever is available from these vulnerable people. With this in mind, approach someone in the grieving family as soon as the times of the visitation and funeral are announced.

Say: "I am aware that there may be evil people who could take advantage of your being away from your home. They have been known to burglarize homes during the visitation and funeral times. With your permission, I'd like to house-sit for you during the hours you're away."

Do: Get to the house on time. Ask if there is anything you can do while you house-sit, such as watering houseplants. Stay the entire time and plan on the time extending well beyond the official hours posted for the visitation. If you are one who wants or needs to be at the visitation or desires to attend the funeral, offer to arrange for a trusted friend to house-sit while you all are away, but only with the permission of the homeowner. Schedule your visitation to the funeral home at a time when there will be someone else at the house.

While this is a task that we'd rather think is quite unnecessary at the time of a death, the reality is that it *is* necessary. Your thoughtfulness in offering to house-sit, even if declined, shows that you are in touch with the family and are willing to do a mundane task to spare the family any additional grief.

 9

Get Out Your Best China

One of the first things we do to mark most significant occasions is to provide food. Birthdays are celebrated with cake and ice cream. New neighbors are often welcomed with a pot of soup from one household, a loaf of bread from another, a plate of cookies from a third. A fellow church member is sick, and the women of the congregation organize a meal. A friend of mine, Richard Obershaw, tagged these parades of food "The Jell-O Brigade."

There are two differing sets of rules for the Jell-O Brigade. If the reason for offering food is a new baby, new home, or illness, the food should be presented on disposable dishes. There are already so many details to keep straight that we prefer not adding the burden of washing and returning a dish. If, on the other hand, the reason is the death of a loved one, present your "Jell-O Brigade" offering on a beautiful family heirloom.

Do: Prepare a dish of food and deliver it to the home of a grieving family. On the assumption that others, too, will have the same idea, select food that can be frozen or refrigerated for later enjoyment. Choose a very nice dish—perhaps cut glass or fine china—to hold your food. Be certain that a tag or piece of masking tape with your name is securely attached.

During the long, lonely days after the funeral, the griever will see your empty dish and know it should be returned, because it clearly is a valuable serving piece. He may comment to you that he has your dish on the counter and really does intend to return it. If he is fortunate, you will invite him in for a cup of coffee. Then he can tell his story one more time and know how much you care.

⌇ 10

Deliver Paper Products

When a death occurs, there are likely to be many visiting family members and friends. There also will be neighbors, friends from church, and others who will kindly stop by with offerings of food to cover meals for several days. (See "Jell-O Brigade" above). The task that is missed, however, is how to serve all those impromptu meals. Visitors won't know where to find table service, and no one needs the extra task of washing dishes during these several hectic days.

Do: As soon as you hear of the death, pack a large grocery bag full of disposable plates, glasses, cups, and cutlery. Ring the doorbell and offer these products to the grieving family to use during these first days of preparation for the funeral.

Say: "I'm so sorry for your loss. I know that you will be receiving food to nourish you and your loved ones, and other people will want to help serve it. I hope that as you use these things you will remember that I am praying for your peace and consolation."

This is an idea that is particularly good for someone who feels somewhat distant from the survivor or awkward speaking words of comfort. As close friends and family continue to use the paper goods, the value of your small gift will be discussed and your care remembered.

ᔕ 11
Sign "The Book"

At almost every death, the funeral directors provide a book to record the signatures of those who attend the visitation or the funeral. Your signature says that you care enough to make that uncomfortable trip across the funeral home threshold. "The book" contains a significant collection of names that is often saved, even cherished, and reread by survivors, sometimes many years later. It also provides a list of people to whom the survivors can send a thank-you note.

Do: Sign "the book." Whether you stop by for a brief visit during the visitation or even if you stay for hours, your signature is a record that you were there. The family and friends who are grieving have so many things on their minds. They are trying to be sociable and emotionally strong, retelling a story for each person who comes by. But they are fighting fatigue. Even if you talk to a survivor, that person may not remember that you were there until weeks later when scanning through the signatures.

Be sure to pen your name legibly. The people who send out thank-you notes may not know you personally, and you can save time and embarrassment by being sure your signature can be deciphered. Write your *complete* name. While the deceased may have known you well by your first name or a nickname, the survivors may not. It is helpful to include a nickname, if that is how the deceased knew you. Example: Robert C. "Charley" Jackson.

If the book has a place for your address, do write it out completely, even if you are confident the family has known your address for decades. It will be very helpful to the survivor who sends out the thank-you notes. Few people have memorized their friends' home addresses.

12
Sign "The Book" by Proxy

Sometimes a death comes when you simply cannot attend the visitation or funeral because of illness, travel, work, or your own family commitment. In that case, it is still possible to have your name in "the book."

Do: Ask someone who is attending to sign your name after he or she signs his or her own. Then follow with an explanation. The explanation may be verbal. I've gone to a funeral home visitation when my husband was out of town on business. He would have attended had he been in town. I signed the book "Carol and Dave Ebeling."

Say: Then, when I had my few moments with a member of the grieving family, I verbally stated, "Dave is out of town on business this week and is so sorry he could not be here today. He sends his sympathies to you along with mine."

Do: The explanation may be written. If you asked someone to sign your name by proxy, immediately send a note explaining the reason for sending a proxy. The note to the surviving spouse of a neighbor who died might read something like this:

Dear Peg,

At the time of Jack's death, we were out of town. But we heard about your loss and asked neighbor Becky to sign our name to the book at the funeral home to let you know we were thinking of you at that time. We want you to know we regret not being able to personally be present and that we were thinking of you.

> Love,
> Carol

〜 13

Remember the Impact of Milestone Occasions

If a friend or acquaintance has experienced the death of a child, it is not just the anniversary of the death day when there is intense grieving. Memories and sadness are also likely to occur when a milestone event would have occurred, had the child lived.

Do: In your mind, connect the age of the child who dies with another child you know. Maybe the child who died was about the same age as a niece or a grandson or a neighbor boy. When a milestone for that living child comes up, it's an appropriate time to connect with the grieving parent or other family member.

Say: "I am remembering _____ (child's name) today, and I am sure you are too. She would be starting kindergarten this week. How well I remember that she was learning her ABCs and already counting to 100. What a beautiful, bright little girl she was. She always lit up a room with her smile, even when she was so sick. I recall the joy she brought to you and to each of us."

Do not be concerned that you will dredge up bad

memories and make someone cry by doing this. Be assured that parents and other survivors never forget a child. Memories rush through their minds every day. Projections of what life would be like had the child not died are happening anyway. Your comments assure the survivors that you, too, are remembering, even years later.

ᴈ 14

Create a New Fund

When 15-year-old Melissa was killed in a tragic auto accident, her friends wanted to do something tangible to remember her beautiful voice and her love of singing. A small contingent of parents of Melissa's friends approached the grieving parents with the idea of establishing a scholarship at the high school in Melissa's name that would pay for one high school student to attend a summer music camp each year.

The death of a person sometimes creates an opportunity to establish a lasting memorial in the form of a fund that either memorializes the deceased or enhances a program that was dear to the deceased. Remember, however, that the fund should never be established without the consent of the grieving family.

Do:

1. The fund should be endowed, that is, have enough principle that the awards made from it can come from the interest earned.

2. The fund should be managed by a foundation or a financial institution, not by an individual or placed as a burden on the family or the school or church administrators. More and more schools and communities have foundations to serve that role. Many banks, especially local ones, will gladly help establish and maintain a trust under the provisions established.

3. Always use an attorney to be sure the fund is established under legal terms for your state and that all systems are in place so the fund will be perpetuated as desired. If not, you may cause the family untold additional future grief if the intention cannot be carried out.

Such a fund could be a burden on the family if not handled properly and legally. Do adequate homework to be sure you have selected a cause the deceased and/or family would appreciate and that it is managed efficiently.

⌒ 15

Return a Treasure

Do you have special memorabilia that you have saved from your relationship with the one who has died? Consider whether any item that you personally have kept such as photo, note, souvenir, or trinket might be given back to the family.

Say: As you share your treasure with them, tell the story that surrounds it. This reassures them that their loved one was special also to you. Your story may even be new information for them to add to their own treasures.

Do: If the memories are in snapshots from your personal collection, you can easily have duplicates made before you give them to the family. Any photo service center will do that. Then add simple captions telling who is in the picture, what is going on, and the date the photo was taken. Frame a single photo or make a small scrapbook to present to the family members. If the memory is a three-dimensional object, a frame shop can encase it in a display frame.

A treasure could be anything: a letter, a matchbook from a special occasion, a yearbook inscription, or a poem written long ago that you had saved and buried in your treasure drawer.

⤳ 16

Offer Specific Help

The temptation when talking to a grieving person is to invite her to call on you for anything that she may need. You mean well. You really would jump at the chance to help in any way. But, what you actually do is give the grieving person one more thing to try to remember. She's likely thinking, Now I have to try to think of something for another person to do for me. It's up to me to remember who wants to feel like a hero. You've given her more to do, not less. Don't be general; be specific.

Here's one scenario. The grieving person is a mom with several small children. Rather than asking if you can provide baby-sitting sometime, try this:

Say: "I want to give you an afternoon to pamper yourself. Here's some bubble bath, a candle, and a magazine. I can care for your children any afternoon next week so you can have four uninterrupted hours to pamper yourself. Which afternoon would work for you?"

Do: Follow through. Adapt as needed to not put more pressure on an intense time. Be creative and persistent in suggesting specific ways you can be of help.

The beauty of this is that you are doing both the work of thinking of some way to help as well as carrying out that help. It will be much appreciated.

⟲ 17

Visit the Terminally Ill

During terminal (or a long-term serious) illness, visits can be very therapeutic for the patient. But you don't want to just drop in. The visit needs to be planned and, normally, needs to be brief. Ask permission of the patient, not just the caregiver, to visit.

Say: Inquire specifically about the patient and the caregiver. You won't cause sadness, but you may allow a release of some emotions. Let the patient tell you about his diagnosis or treatment. Don't tell him. Reminisce with the patient. Share photo albums from days/years gone by.

Retell stories of short-sheeting a camp counselor, building a tree house, decorating Christmas cookies.

Do: Touch is comforting. Hold a hand. Stroke an arm, a forehead, or a cheek. Limit visiting time. Two 20-minute visits are often better than one 40-minute visit. Read familiar Bible passages, like the Twenty-third Psalm, or sing favorite songs. Pray the Lord's Prayer. These familiar things are comforting even for someone too ill to concentrate on the text, and the power of God's Word will carry through.

Adapt familiar activities so that the patient can enjoy them under the new circumstances. For instance, you might take along an audio book for listening rather than a printed book that would have to be read.

∽ 18

Terminal Illness—How to Say "Good-bye"

In many respects, having a terminal diagnosis is a blessing. We know that everyone will die, but we behave like we'll live forever. Our busy lives become excuses for not visiting relatives. Some people have jobs, or change jobs, that uproot them and send them hundreds or thousands of miles away from friends and family. It is even easier to avoid contact when there have been tensions in a relationship. Then a doctor finds a malignant lump or a blood sample tests positive for a terminal illness. Suddenly the world turns upside down, and our priorities change.

When we know with a degree of certainty that time is short, there are things we want to do and people we need to see. We must put closure on this life as we make final spiritual preparations for eternity in heaven. We repent of our sins. We make confession to our pastor. We receive absolution from him as from Christ Himself. We receive the true body and blood of Christ in the Lord's Supper. In addition, there are four end-of-life tasks that make that transition to eternity easier. As a friend, you can initiate each of them.

Say: "I love you." If you have a close, loving relationship with the patient, you can be the first to use these words. If not, try to discover if there are people who need to say or hear these words. They may find visiting very difficult; perhaps you can begin with telephone contact.

Say: "I forgive you." As you learn about people from the past, listen for names of people who have not been around for a while. Is there some unpleasant history? Talk about the joy that comes from sharing the Gospel by forgiving someone. Inquire if you can provide pen and paper to write a note of forgiveness, or offer to be the secretary that writes such a dictated letter.

Say: "Will you forgive me?" The patient may know people he has wronged sometime in his life without apologizing. Talk about the peace that results from receiving forgiveness from someone with whom you have unfinished business. You may again offer to initiate such a contact.

Say: "Good-bye." Those of us walking around with reasonably healthy bodies find it hard to understand that someone would want to talk about his death. One of the many things that I learned from all the patients I met while serving as director of the local hospice program is that terminally ill patients need to know their loved ones will not be surprised by their death. One way to ensure that is to let the patient say good-bye to family and friends. That removes the worry that someone may think doctors have a cure for this disease. Some people find comfort in talking about their death a lot, others need mention it only once.

Do: Suggest hospice care when you hear that the doctors have diagnosed a terminal illness. Some doctors automatically do this themselves. Others wait for the patient or family to request it. Hospice care includes a full interdisciplinary team of professionals and volunteers to help the patient live out the rest of his life in whatever way he most wants. It often means staying at home rather than being rushed back and forth to the hospital. It means giving time off to caregivers before they are totally exhausted. It means providing special attention for the children. It means follow-up care for a year after the death occurs. It means the privilege of declining some of the list of services I just mentioned, so that the patient and family, rather than the disease process, are in control.

⁓ 19
Pew Partners

After the funeral a grieving person faces an almost insurmountable task—going to church. This is especially true when the funeral itself was held at the church. Walking into the sanctuary again and seeing the exact space in which the casket stood just days earlier can be overwhelming, especially if it means sitting in a pew all alone.

Say: "This Sunday, would you honor us by sitting with our family in church?" or "May I sit with you this morning?"

Do: Invite the survivor in person or by phone a day or two before the worship service. Or, if you prefer, simply get to church early on a Sunday and wait near the coatrack or any place you're likely to see the person when he/she arrives. Start a conversation in the narthex, and then just walk in together. Another option is simply to see where the person is sitting and quietly join him/her in the same pew.

Worship is such an important aspect of a Christian's life. The longer one waits to return to regular worship after a funeral, the more difficult it is likely to become. You can help by intentionally making that transition a little less lonely.

∽ 20

Be a Prayer Warrior

Prayer is powerful. "Do not be anxious about anything, but in everything, by prayer and petition, with thanksgiving, present your requests to God" (Philippians 4:6). Even in his grief, Jonah could declare, "When my life was ebbing away, I remembered You, LORD, and my prayer rose to You, to Your holy temple" (Jonah 2:7).

Say: "I've been talking to the Lord about you."

Do: Be certain you have actually done so. Pray with the survivor/surviving family. Help her/him know that the Father sent His own Son to die on the cross to forgive their sins and bear the burden of their grief.

Some congregations have prayer chains through which prayer requests are channeled. If that is true in your area, ask the grieving person if you can add her and her needs to the prayers of your group. Ask if there is anything specific you and your fellow prayer warriors can include in your petitions to the heavenly Father.

∽ 21

Just Sit There

You've arrived at the funeral home. Now what? You are struck with the grief that is being felt by all who have experienced this loss. You don't know what to say, but you want to be there. That's okay.

Say: "I don't know what to say, but I'm going to just sit here so you don't feel so alone."

Do: Sit. Pray. Observe. Hug.

Many people know that the shortest verse in the Bible is John 11:35, "Jesus wept." Few contemplate its meaning, that He who is true God is also true man. Jesus Christ had human feelings of grief. And in this situation, when Jesus was with his friends Mary and Martha after their brother, Lazarus, had died, He didn't say anything or do anything. He sat down and cried with them. This shows us a God in Christ who bears our burdens and carries our sorrows. And in the same way He enables us to "mourn with those who mourn" (Romans 12:15).

〜 22

Be a Sounding Board

Retelling "the story" is healthy for most mourners. Talking about her loved one, the illness and/or death, works like a saturated sponge. Each time the story is told, a little more pain is squeezed out, and the need to talk about the details decreases. It is as if she is painting a picture of the incident.

Do: Create opportunities for a mourner to talk. Encourage conversation about what has happened. Discuss fragile feelings and anything else relating to the one who died. Encourage the mourner to do the grief work. Friends can give hugs, write caring notes, visit, and pray.

Only the mourner can cry his own tears, scream his own screams, live through his own long, lonely nights. By doing so, he reidentifies himself without his loved one.

Say: "How about having lunch with me on Tuesday?"

Eventually, the picture in her mind's eye is ready to hang on the wall and to be looked at whenever she wants. Once it is hung, she no longer needs to carry it around and be burdened by it and controlled by the past.

∽ 23

Extend an Invitation

In time, gently invite the mourner back into activities. She may lack desire and courage to go out alone. Accept her decision that the time or specific activity isn't right for now. Then gently invite her on another occasion for something else.

Do: Whenever she returns to social activity, treat her as a normal person. Public displays of pity destroy self-respect. Offer to go with her if it is an activity you both enjoy. Make intentional efforts to reassure her that she needs to do this.

Say: "Let's do this together. You're in charge of the clock, but it's been awhile since either of us has gone out to _____."

∽ 24
Be a Good Listener

Take time to listen. In person, over the phone, or even by e-mail, listening tells the grieving person that her grief is valid. Her thoughts, while they may seem repetitive and even rambling, are in need of moving from her innermost spirit into the public. You become the public. A listener is needed. You are the listener.

Do: Make eye contact. Don't look down or away. Reach out and touch her hand, hug him if it feels natural. Tell her with your eyes and facial expressions that you care about what's happening in her life. Let him know that you are listening willingly. Even the most reserved person will usually accept the genuine expression of affection. Don't rush to fill silences. Loving silence in the form of listening can be the greatest gift and comfort of all. Allowing someone to empty his overflowing cup of cares into your keeping, and sharing his feelings for a while, takes the terrible sting and aloneness out of any problem.

Say: Rephrase comments to check for understanding. Recap incidents so the speaker can pick up from a point of distraction or tears. Mostly, say very little. Listen with all your heart.

⌒ 25

Acknowledge One's Presence

After a funeral it may seem awkward to talk to the grieving person. After all, you can ask, "How're you doing?" only so many times. But saying nothing has the effect of the grieving person becoming a nonperson in your life. So your challenge is to talk to the person as often as you would have prior to the death of that person's loved one.

Do: Reflect on the amount of communication you had with an individual before the loss. Then try to maintain that level of communication, even trying to discuss similar topics.

Say: "What quilt pattern are you working on now?" or "Wasn't that Cubs game yesterday great?" or "Could you use some help going through the tools in the garage?"

Any topic is fair game. Mix references to the death and related activities with everyday topics that were always a part of your conversations. Enjoy small talk again. Everything doesn't have to be serious. Laugh together. Say and do routine things together just like before. Help restart a little normalcy into the person's life.

⟿ 26

Help, Save, Comfort, and Defend

One of the prayers often read in Christian churches includes this petition to our heavenly Father: "Help, save, comfort, and defend us, gracious Lord." In simple yet direct words we ask the Lord to take four actions on our behalf. These same four words can remind you of actions you, too, can take.

Do:

Help the grieving person through this valley.

Save some time to listen.

Provide *comfort* with hugs or your simple presence.

Defend the person's right to grieve in her own time and way.

Say: "When I pray for you, I find myself using the same words I hear in the common prayers at church from time to time, 'Help, save, comfort, and defend us, gracious Lord.' When you hear those words, be assured that the Lord does, in fact, help, save, comfort, and defend you."

Those same four words could be the core of your comments to a grieving person at a funeral home. If you can think of little to say, try, "May our Lord help, save, comfort, and defend you."

⤳ 27

Do a Calendar Check

At the time of a death, everything in the grieving family's life comes to a halt. The devastation of a loss, even one that was inevitable or expected, still demands all the survivor's emotional and cognitive energy. The rest of the world keeps going, though, and someone needs to relieve the family of the responsibility to reschedule mundane tasks.

Do: Visit a family member as soon as possible at a residence or place of business. Have a pencil and pad with you. Invite the grieving folks to check their memory or calendar for anything that can be canceled or postponed during the next 30 days:

Medical or dental appointments

Books or videos to be returned

Service calls someone is scheduled to make at the home

Gifts that need to be delivered for a birthday or wedding

A traffic fine to be paid

Dry cleaning to be picked up

Consider other possibilities

Say: "I'm so sorry for your loss. You will need to devote all of your attention and energy to making funeral arrangements and talking to family and friends. If you could take a few minutes to look at your calendar, I'll take responsibility to notify any businesses of your _____'s death and get your appointments canceled or tasks completed."

You can help the grieving individual or family deal with routine tasks when the days and weeks are anything but routine. Be sure to write detailed notes about every contact you make. At a time when they can focus, sit down with the people and your notes to inform them of all the contacts you made, all the tasks completed, and anything that will need their follow-up in the future. Give them everything in writing so they do not have to remember the details.

↬ 28

Talk to the Children

Children are often ignored. In fact, at most visitations, children are overlooked. They may be off in a room where they can play or watch videos. They may have been intentionally left at home or with a child-care provider. But children grieve too. They have fears and memories, and thoughts that need a way to be expressed.

Do: If children are visible at all, talk to them. Sit on a chair or get your eyes down to their level to carry on a conversation.

Say: "I'll always remember your Aunt Peggy for the time she drove through a terrible snow storm to bring my family a meal when I had surgery. What will you remember about your aunt?" or "Your brother loved the challenge of computer games. Did you ever play with him?"

Children always assume the worst when they do not know the truth. They almost always feel some guilt for someone's death, even when they are far removed from the situation. By giving them opportunities to talk, you increase the likelihood that they will express their feelings in such a way that you or other adults can learn what their perceptions are. Talk to the children.

〜 29

Throw Away the Clock

Many people will offer advice about how and when to resume social activities and to make personal decisions. There will be one person suggesting the time has come to get out and become involved at the same time another person will urge holding back for a later, more appropriate time. Reassure her/him that the mourning clock ticks at many speeds and without rules. Although it is painful, the process of grieving is a friend, not an enemy. It helps get us back to a state of balance physically and emotionally. The anger, fear, guilt, despair, and loneliness usually ebb and flow for years.

Say: "You must feel as if this pain will never end. Only you can decide when the time is right to go places, to make decisions, to clean out closets."

Do: Show that you understand that grief lingers on long after the funeral. Concentrate on the present, however, not how they may feel several years from now. To the bereaved, each day can seem like an eternity.

∽ 30

Mark Your Calendar with the Anniversary Date

While the dates of the death and funeral of someone may not be important to you, those dates are indelibly etched in the mind of the grieving person. While visiting with an aunt recently, we were rebuilding a family tree. We asked, "Do you know what year Grandma Emma died?" Without hesitation she said, "March 18, 1945. I'll never forget that date. I was just 16."

It's especially meaningful, then, when someone else outside the family does not forget that significant date either.

Do: If you jot the date down on your personal or family calendar, perhaps you'll remember a year later to make a phone call or send a note on the first anniversary of the loved one's death. Maybe just seeing the person in church will give you an opportunity to say something. Often a survivor puts flowers on the altar at that time. Use the reminder to make a personal connection.

Say: If you don't see the person, send a note. Here's an example:

Dear Ruth,

I recall that this is the week of the anniversary of the death of your dear husband, Fred. I miss seeing him at church, where we were always greeted by a hearty handshake and smile.

This has to be a time of sadness for you, too, as you reach this anniversary date. I'm thankful for your faith that sustains you. Be assured that neither you nor Fred is forgotten.

Carol

↪ 31
Light Up a Life

Many communities have an organization that puts up a Christmas tree in a public place and invites members of the community to make a donation to the organization in memory of someone who has died. In my hometown of Bloomington, Indiana, we initiated a "Light Up a Life" program when I was director of hospice. A tall Christmas tree was planted on the courthouse square. A few years later, we added a second smaller tree for children's names. The ceremony soon became so popular that the lighting of those trees on Thanksgiving Friday became the community launching of the Christmas season. If there is such a program where you live, it is a good opportunity to memorialize a person who has died and support a local charity at the same time.

Do: Make a notation on your personal or family calendar of the names and dates of people who die during the year. Then, when the season comes for you to send money and names of the people you are memorializing, your list will be ready.

Say: Notify a survivor that one of the lights on that tree is burning for a loved one. Our hospice agency presents every donor with an acknowledgement card and an optional engraved Christmas ornament to give to the survivors. If nothing is provided, make a point to tell a survivor that you remembered the deceased person and you did light up a life.

Holidays, especially Christmas, are very hard on grieving family members. This way, you can light up their lives by demonstrating that you, too, are remembering their loved one and consoling them in their loss.

∽ 32

Remind Him of His Baptism

There are many situations that make it impossible to understand the usual message of comfort. It might be that the survivor has suffered a stroke or is in advanced stages of Alzheimer's disease. It could be that you want to comfort a trauma patient who is in deep pain physically as well as spiritually. Maybe there have been multiple deaths, and the level of grief and numbness is even higher than normal. Perhaps there has been a crime, a suicide, a school shooting. There is one message that we can offer that may be remembered and cherished even under all these circumstances. That is the message of God's love in Christ. On the cross, Jesus "took up our infirmities and carried our sorrows . . . and by His wounds we are healed" (Isaiah 53:4–5). By faith in Him, we have the forgiveness of sins and everlasting life. These blessings are sealed to us in the Sacrament of Holy Baptism, where we were baptized in the name of the triune God. When we make the sign of the cross and repeat the words "In the name of the Father and of the Son and of the Holy Spirit," we remember our Baptism. We can remind others of their Baptism with these words as well.

Say: " 'In the name of the Father and of the Son and of the Holy Spirit.' That is how your life as God's child began; that is how it is today; and that it is how it will be forever."

33

Suicide Is Haunting

Suicide carries with it the added dimensions of shame, anger, and guilt. Close friends and family members often spend weeks and months reviewing every conversation, every contact, every behavior that preceded the death to determine if there had been warning signs that they should have noticed. They need to know that no one who decides to kill himself can be kept alive by someone else being vigilant. They also need to be assured that they are different people than those who die by their own hand. Surviving family members often worry that they, too, will cave in under pressure. As with many crime scenes, suicide scenes may bear unpleasant evidence of the chosen method of death. This sight often haunts the family for months or years to come. Some people find it necessary to move from their house if death occurred there.

Do: Help clean up the area after police finish their work. Or, if that has been done or is unnecessary, offer to stay with the survivor until close family arrives. In the weeks and months that follow the funeral, continue to talk about your positive memories of the deceased, just as you would if death had come from natural causes.

Say: "I know that you have a lot to deal with, but I want you to remember that John was more than the desperate man you are grieving. I remember how kind he was to me when _____."

∾ 34

Traumatic Death

Survivors of traumatic deaths have the same spiritual, financial, physical, cultural/ethnic, psychological, and social needs of other grievers, but often with several added dimensions of pain. In some cases, these survivors have witnessed the death and themselves been in danger. Homicide survivors fear that the perpetrator will come after them, especially if they come forward to cooperate with the police. Those who have experienced a natural disaster experience fear or anxiety over the possibility of a reoccurrence claiming their lives or the lives of additional loved ones.

It is important for trauma survivors to feel that they have regained some control over their lives and their personal environment. The trauma often leaves them feeling victimized by someone or some circumstance. Some needs are the same whether traumatic or natural death is involved: the need to comprehend the death, both intellectually and emotionally; the need to experience the grief; the need to mourn; and the need for an unspecified time to adjust to life without the deceased.

Do: In the case of homicide, offer to go along to police headquarters for official questioning, processing, and paperwork. The process itself is frightening for most people, for whom the police station is a scary place. The sense of victimization may decrease as the survivor realizes that he has the power to help bring about justice and stop the perpetrator from repeating his crime.

There are some circumstances of death that are truly so horrible that everyone is overwhelmed. My son knows a family man who befriended a homeless man. The homeless man rewarded this kind man by raping his wife and cutting her into pieces. What words of comfort do you use in a situation like this? Platitudes like "It must have been God's time for her to enter eternity" don't work. We know with certainty that God does not choose evil for His faithful followers. Rote words often take on new meaning, however, when our minds are spinning. In the Kyrie portion of our Lutheran liturgy we sing, "Lord, have mercy." The pastor responds, "Help, save, comfort, and defend us, gracious Lord." That pretty much says it all.

Do: Send a note that can be read once or often. Keep the message brief. Grief clouds the mind, and a lengthy letter might be too exhausting to be appreciated until much later. In that letter, make reference to familiar words of comfort.

Say: "I can't imagine how you feel with these horrible circumstances. Each week as we worship together, we pray for the Lord's mercy as part of our Divine Service. And now these familiar words are my prayer, that the Lord will 'help, save, comfort, and defend' you."

⟿ 35

Take a Candle with You

Walking into the funeral home is a daunting experience for most people. We are particularly saddened when a child dies. There are many emotions, not the least of which is the sense that we adults have failed to properly care for the young child.

Do: Purchase a candle and attach a card with a ribbon. On the card, write "Home Sweet Home: The light of your life is with Jesus, the light of the world."

Say: "I have not had to send a child ahead of me to heaven. It is my prayer that this candle will remind you that Jesus, the light of the world, has prepared a place for him. That same Jesus is with you too."

The family may keep the candle as a tangible reminder of the salvation that is ours through Jesus. They may burn it on special days or the anniversary of the child's death. It may be placed in the child's bedroom with other keepsakes. We don't need to know how it is used, but we can be quite sure that seeing the candle will remind them of your Christian love for them.

36
Journal with Jesus

Grief seems to go on forever. It is often difficult to mark improvements and find hope that the future will ever be brighter. Suggest that your grieving friend write out her thoughts and feelings as a way of expressing not only the pain, but also the moments of hope. The journal should not be a rigid part of each day, but rather an opportunity to record a highlight. With some entries, suggest writing a Bible verse that comes to mind, a plea to God for a special need, or a way in which she could see God's hand at work.

Do: Provide a special journal with blank pages. Include one of many available brief lists or booklets that match biblical references with certain circumstances.

These "Where to turn when ..." lists can be very helpful in grief, when even someone who has committed many Bible passages to memory may have trouble recalling the location of favorite texts.

Say: "I know that it seems that your life may never be happy again. Please consider writing some of your deepest sorrows as well as lighter moments when they come. Date each entry. As time goes by, you can reread this little journal and watch the progress you and the Lord together are making as you walk this most difficult path. It is my prayer that what troubles you this month will be less difficult three months from now. It might give you strength to discover that there are reasons for thanksgiving even during these early weeks."

◒ 37

Responding to "If Only"

A normal response to death is to relive the past and look for indications that something might have been done to prevent it. It is rare, indeed, when a survivor doesn't continue this mental exercise for weeks and even months. You may hear comments like, "If only I had ..." or "I wish I had not ..."

Often we interpret these expressions as guilt feelings. If we react by saying, "You mustn't feel guilty; you did everything you could," we unintentionally tell him that he should not have those feelings. Going over the past until it begins to make some sense brings with it a small sense of control. It helps, too, to make the horrible unreal situation more acceptable.

There is a difference between guilt and regret that can be useful. *Guilt* is how we feel when we intentionally hurt someone. *Regret* is the feeling we have when hindsight tells us that we could have handled things differently. Don't be too quick to suggest that he should stop going over the details. Probably in time, the events will make more sense to him and he can set aside his regrets.

Do: Listen carefully and patiently as he talks about the events. Don't jump in to tell him he "mustn't feel" a certain way. He already feels out of control; he doesn't need to be told he has no right to his feelings.

Say: "What could you have done differently?" "Then what might have happened?" This may take several weeks or months. Be patient. If the feeling of guilt is based on reality, professional help may be needed.

⤳ 38

Make Room for Laughter

Conversation should not be limited to serious, sorrowful phrases. Ordinary, even cheerful, topics can help. This is true especially as the person moves closer to resolving grief and rebuilding life without the loved one. Forced cheerfulness, however, will make both of you uncomfortable.

Do: Blend topics of conversation rather than focus only on somber ones. Then when you see evidence that she is enjoying a joke, the silly antics of a small child, a sweet memory, comment that it's good to see a smile.

Say: "It is so good to see that for a brief time you are able to feel lighthearted again. I know that there are many times when tears fall on your pillow at 2 A.M., but I want you to know that I think your strength is improving."

The caution here is to not suggest that you want your friend to wear a phony happy face for your sake. Rather, acknowledge how difficult you know it is to forget the grief, but that the smile suggested to you that the grief is becoming a more natural part of life, rather than the only focus.

〰 39
Sing

There are certain hymns that have always been associated with funerals. The appropriateness of them, however, does not require us to limit the music we choose. Everyone has a favorite hymn. As with many parents, mine lived hundreds of miles from me until they were advanced in age. When they moved nearby, my mother no longer taught kindergarten in a Lutheran school or three-year-olds in Sunday school. But that was a significant part of her life. For the funeral, we prepared a medley of Christian children's songs for the whole congregation to sing as a celebration of God's grace in Mom's life.

Do: Choose songs or hymns that express the faith and life of the person who died. If you're responsible for planning the funeral, include those that are especially meaningful.

Say: "_____ sang and listened to hymns of the church. Music was always meaningful and important to him/her. Sing those hymns with us as we recall the mercies of our heavenly Father."

Your singing—or having a soloist perform the songs—says it all. People close to your loved one will understand the appropriateness of the selections.

⌒ 40

When Your Pastor Dies

The death of a pastor makes a strong spiritual and emotional impact on the whole congregation. He has been the confidant for many families as they have struggled through personal issues. He has shared the joy of weddings and new babies, as well as the sorrow of grave illness and death. He has helped many young men and women find their calling as professional church worker, and he has encouraged everyone to discover and fulfill God's plan for their lives. To some people, he has also been a close personal friend. He has been the spiritual father of this congregational family. Depending on how long he has served the congregation, the personal family that survives might extend into several generations.

A large portion of the congregation will go through the same tasks of grief that any family experiences because they are a family. It is critically important that there be an open invitation for opportunities to commemorate the pastor's life. He may have been counseling with individuals who have not worshiped for some time. They will feel despair over losing their stronghold back into the fold, while others in the congregation will not be aware of this relationship.

Do: Include everyone in planning a post-funeral get-together, but check plans with the widow and children. They may prefer to have a smaller, intimate group support them on the day of the funeral. Ask if a separate event for the congregation should come later. Remember that you do not own the pastor's family; this is their personal time.

Say: "We all will deeply miss Pastor, but we don't want to interfere with your personal family time. Please tell us if anything we suggest for the congregation is crossing that line."

Do: Plan a meal or other fellowship time for congregational members to tell their stories. Encourage people to bring pictures and other memorabilia from times they shared with the pastor. If he was active in youth ministry, some of the former youth may want to reenact events that happened as part of youth gatherings or service trips.

Do: Commemorate his life with a display. Choose a large bulletin board in the church narthex, fellowship hall, or school all-purpose room. Using ribbon, place a heart on the board and provide pens and small pads of paper on a nearby table. Invite people to write favorite memories of the years they knew the pastor. Leave the display up for several weeks and then assemble all the papers in a scrapbook to give the family.

The bulletin board will help each person who writes a memory, but it also will help those who take time to read other peoples' memories. Another version of this idea is to provide a blank book in which people can write their memories. This idea, however, limits how many people can enjoy the writings at any given time.

⤳ 41

Look beyond the Brave Front

Surface actions don't always reflect inner feelings. Many adults, especially men, have been taught that crying is a sign of weakness. A man once said, "I slept like a baby the night my son died. I slept for an hour, then got up and cried, slept for an hour, then got up and cried." Sometimes people fear that once tears come, they may never stop. A third reason for the brave front is simply that the circumstances do not allow the griever time to cry before needing to be strong again for a task that is waiting. St. Augustine, a great poet of Christian antiquity, wrote after the death of his mother, "I didn't cry then, nor at the funeral, but later alone one night, I let the tears flow making a pillow for my heart."

Say: "I know how hard it can be to share feelings with someone else. Perhaps you could write a letter to _____ as if she were still alive. Tell her what you are doing, what you feel, how different your life is now."

Say: "I really miss _____. He was a special person. But my missing him can't compare with how much you must miss him. Tell me what that's like."

Attempting to avoid the emotional pain of grief leaves the door open for trouble in the future. It always waits, and it often resurfaces at surprising moments when a support system is no longer available.

～ 42

Share the Gospel Message

A seven-year-old boy on a field trip to the St. Louis Zoo was standing with his first-grade classmates and chaperones. A drunken man, driving recklessly, lost control of his car, striking a man and killing young Luke. The 350-seat sanctuary was crowded with over 600 people on the day of his funeral. His classmates sat with their parents in the front pews and sang "Shine, Jesus Shine," one of Luke's favorite songs. At the gravesite, 500 red and white balloons were launched, each carrying the biblical message "Let the little children come to Me."

The sister of the driver who killed the boy watched quietly from the sidelines and then tapped the pastor on the shoulder. With a troubled face, she told him that she thought most people would not want her there, but she wondered if she could speak with Luke's parents. This was done. She asked them to forgive her brother, and the parents responded with an embrace and words of reassurance. They told her that God forgives sins for Christ's sake, and He enables us to forgive those who do wrong against us. On the basis of Christ's atoning death on the cross, they could and did forgive the man who killed their child. The newspaper granted front-page coverage to the details of how the Gospel was shared that day.

Do: Recognize that the witnesses to this death are emotionally numb. Sometimes when children discover that feelings hurt this much, they will "refuse" to feel anything at all. Encourage the parents to take their children to the funeral home so that they can begin to experience their grief.

This teacher and family worked together to involve the classmates through singing Luke's favorite Gospel song and then through the Gospel-sharing balloon launch. What a beautiful way of beginning the mourning process of making their grief public.

Say: "I know that right now you don't want to remember what you saw at the zoo. You don't want to think about how sad you feel that Luke has died. It is important for all of us, however, to be together right now.

We need to help Luke's family also, and the best way to do that is to share how much Jesus loves him. This is also a very good chance for us to tell other people about Jesus and His love."

43

Sign the Casket

Emotions are neither right nor wrong; they just are. When the drunken driver killed seven-year-old Luke during broad daylight and in full view of his classmates, his parents looked for ways to connect his classmates tangibly to the reality of his death. Children under the age of eight find it difficult to accept the permanence of death, so any physical ritual that is included as part of the final days will be important. In this case, mourners were invited to sign the casket as they said their final good-bye. Perhaps touching the casket itself helped children and adults to begin their grief journey.

Do: Provide permanent markers that will allow indelible signatures on the surface of the casket. Have someone make a small sign inviting people to sign their names or even a brief memory of the deceased. Members of the family may want to be among the first to sign the casket as examples of what might be written and to "give permission" to do so.

Say: "Perhaps you have already signed the guest book that we will keep. We also invite you to use a marker and sign the casket as a final farewell to _____."

Other mourners will read the names and messages that are on the casket. Some may be Gospel-based, some special memories, others simply signatures. Whatever is written, the process of touching the casket and viewing the body a few extra moments will help them to move along in the necessary process of experiencing their grief.

44

Missing Person

When a person is missing, the grief is different from a death. There is no answer. There are only questions that compound and continue until the lost is found—dead or alive. In our community, Jill Behrman, a 19-year-old hometown college student, went bicycle riding in the early morning hours of May 30, 2000. She didn't return home. Her bike was found five miles from where she was riding. As this book goes to press, Jill is still missing.

Do: Participate in the search. The police consider many missing-person cases routine and no search is started for 24 or 48 hours. But the family can search—and volunteers are needed to walk fields, go door-to-door, or do whatever seems most likely to turn up evidence.

Say: "I will help in any way I can. I have read accounts of similar situations where people posted fliers in storefronts, told their story through the media, and engaged the help of truckers to spread fliers. Maybe it would help if I simply answered your phone for a few hours while you try to rest."

Missing children and adults create even more trauma than many deaths. It is grief without ending, like tearing open a wound every day.

∽ 45
Present a Guest Book

Time goes by so slowly for critically and terminally ill patients. Memory can be dimmed by medication, pain, or the illness itself. Caregivers who alternate or who are given a few hours of time off by a friend want to know who visited and what was done. If you are about to visit someone, especially if the diagnosis is new, buy or make a guest book for the patient and the caregivers. If you have the interest and skills, decorate it with graphics reflecting the patient's interests.

Do: Personally deliver the guest book. But before you do, make the first entry. Include the date and time of the visit, your name as a guest in their home, and a description of the activity. Your first entry might read something like this:

> Date: June 24
> Time: 2:00 P.M.
> Guest: Carol Ebeling
> Activity: Came for a visit and presented
>   this guest book

Say: "I brought you this guest book so you can keep track of the people who come to visit you. I invite you to leave it out where you can reach it, so you can ask anyone, even caregivers, to 'sign in.' It will also give you a written record of those visits, and you might enjoy reading through it once in a while."

The guest book concept has value for a grieving person as well. Many people likely signed "the book" at the funeral home (see ideas 11 and 12). Having another guest book at the residence of the grieving person can add comfort to that person as well, reminding him of people who have stopped by or called.

∽ 46

Videotape Thoughts and Memories

In many cases a terminally ill patient is experiencing weakness and frailty of the body, but the mind is racing with thoughts. Helping to get those thoughts expressed verbally or in writing can be a once-in-a-lifetime gift. When Barbara, a young mother of three, was dying, one of her wishes was to prepare a book of thoughts for each milestone event in her children's future, especially her daughter's wedding (her daughter was nine years old at the time). A friend with a video camera offered to help.

Say: Talk openly with the patient. Inquire about the thoughts that are racing through her mind. Probe for a specific idea you could help capture. Listen extensively—

even take notes to help random thought take shape. Propose a plan that you could manage.

Do: Make all the arrangements to get it done as quickly as possible. If it means videotaping the patient saying words of encouragement to be viewed years later, help the patient look her very best in front of the camera. Do the taping at the patient's optimal time of the day. When the taping and editing are completed, take it to the patient for a premier showing. Be sure the tape is labeled, make a backup, and assure the patient that it will be delivered to the intended audience.

Videotapes make wonderful memories for families. If you are ministering to a terminally ill person, consider producing a videotape. From the moment we know that a baby is coming, adult members of a family begin to imagine the future as parents, grandparents, aunts, and uncles. From the moment we know a death is coming, it is especially important to the patient to have peace that those children will grow up with at least a few clear memories of them.

◦ 47

Stories on Tape for Kids

A parent or grandparent can be remembered long after death by providing his or her voice as the storyteller of favorite books of a child or grandchild. You can help by setting up the equipment and taking care of the details.

Say: When you visit a dying patient, ask about any books that she/he likes to read to a child. Suggest that you audiotape the patient reading the books. That way, the child can listen to the voice over and over for years to come.

Do: Find the books. Bring them to the patient. As you start the taping, invite the patient to say a few words about the story and how special it is to him or her. Have a small bell ready to ring on the tape every time a page is turned. Then the listener will know when to turn pages.

If time permits, a small collection of these could be produced. Label the tapes clearly, including the date the tape was made and the name of the person whose voice is recorded. Be sure the intended listener gets the tapes.

⤳ 48
Schedule Time-out for a Caregiver

Anyone who cares for a seriously ill patient finds himself almost totally consumed by responsibility to the patient. Many caregivers find themselves homebound with the patient, deprived of sleep, and on duty 24 hours a day, seven days a week. One way to show your love and care is to offer to take on those responsibilities for a few hours at a time so the caregiver can have a small reprieve.

Say: "I've noticed how deeply you care for
_____. I admire the commitment you have made to care for him/her literally around the clock. If you

would trust me to care for him/her for a short while, I would come to your home while you get away for a little while. You might shop, get your hair done, or go to a church service."

Do: Get to the home on time. Listen intently to directions. Avoid rushing the caregiver off. Take the time to grasp the list of things you are to watch for and to learn how to care for the patient the way the caregiver does. While on duty, make a list of the things you did and the time you did them. For instance, if you give a certain medication, note the dose and the time given.

When the caregiver returns, allow plenty of time to talk. Go over your list of tasks completed with the caregiver. If at all possible, schedule the next time you'll be available to do the same thing. Perhaps it can be a regularly scheduled support while the need is there.

↼ 49

Exercise

Exercise is a wonderful stress reducer. Talk to her about the benefits of exercise. If you share interest in a sport, suggest doing it together. If neither of you swim, play racquetball, golf, tennis, or another individual or partner sport, take a walk together. Fast-walking an hour a day can decrease stress by 25 percent. Some sports, like walking, have the added benefit of providing an opportunity for conversation.

Do: Schedule physical exercise that you and your grieving friend can do together. It will be physically good for both of you. It might provide conversation time as well.

Say: "I haven't been keeping as active as I should. Would you be willing to walk with me (or swim, play tennis, etc.)? It might help you walk off some of the stress of coping with your grief, and I know it would help me with my life."

～ 50

Is It Too Late to Call?

No matter how much time has passed since the death or trauma occurred, be sure to call or visit. He will appreciate knowing that you care and usually will understand that it was difficult for you to come. I know several teachers who admitted to hiding behind classroom and washroom doors at school because they failed to make condolence visits during the summer. When school reopened in the fall, they felt it was too late to approach the child who was then in another classroom. Once they spoke to the grieving child, both teacher and student were able to move on.

Do: Send a note, call, or make a personal visit no matter how much time has elapsed since the death or trauma occurred.

Say: "I'm so sorry I didn't express my sympathy sooner. I have been praying for your peace and comfort, but I had the mistaken notion that I couldn't speak with you unless I had something brilliant to say. Please accept my apology as well as my condolence."

 51

Remember the First Anniversary

In idea 30 I suggested that you mark on your calendar the date of the death of someone. If you were actually doing one of these 52 suggestions each week for a year, this would be the time to plan a way to observe the first anniversary of a death. Make it simple, but make it meaningful.

Do: Reflect on what the grieving person might miss about the person who died. If he was a golfer, have a florist prepare a bouquet with a golfing motif. If she was famous for her egg salad at church potlucks, deliver an egg salad dish to her daughter. If it was a five-year-old who drowned a year ago, color a picture as a six-year-old might and write, "I love you, Mommy" on it; give it to the family with a refrigerator magnet.

Say: "This date will always be a bittersweet one for you and all who loved _____. I'm aware of the changes that have impacted your life throughout the year, and I thank God for the strength He has given you. This gift is to celebrate his life and yours!"

The grieving person is nearing a milestone—surviving one full year without a special loved one. You will not make the grief worse by recognizing the occasion. Rather, your words and actions will underscore your love and caring because you remembered. You remembered the person who died. You remembered the person who grieves.

⤿ 52

Support Group

Grief shared is grief diminished. There are grief support groups in many communities that are sponsored by hospices, churches, and local branches of national causes. One such group is Compassionate Friends, a support group for parents who have buried a child, whether that child is an infant or middle-aged adult. If you are interested in a particular group, and one is not organized in your area, you can contact the National Self-Help Clearing House. They publish a comprehensive book that lists by category the self-help groups throughout the United States. This book also provides information on forming support groups.

Do: Risking change is always difficult, and even more so during grief. If someone you know expresses interest in a support group, offer to accompany him to the meetings. He will not be as lonely, and you have conversation opportunities before and after each group meeting.

Say: "There are support groups available in town for people who are walking the same difficult road that you are. Attending these meetings can be very hard too. Would you be interested in trying a group? I would be willing to go as your partner."

If your congregation could offer space and leadership for a support group, follow the suggested guidelines and add the Christian dimensions of Word and prayer. Yours will be a far more effective group.

Two Final Reminders

First Reminder: Three Terms

Early in this book, I defined three terms that are often used or misused interchangeably: bereavement, grief, and mourning. Here they are again:

You lose something.

This is *bereavement*—the act of being bereft or cut off from something.

You react to it internally.

This is *grief*—your personal, physical, emotional, and mental reaction to the loss.

If you are fortunate, people let you share your grief publicly.

This is *mourning*—grief made public. Without mourning, grief often leads to relational and other personal problems.

All of us have, or will have, reasons to grieve. But, even more often, we become the "public" when someone else is mourning. Thus we search for ways to witness to our faith and serve those who are grieving. It's natural that we feel tension between our desire to show sympathy for grieving individuals and our own shyness or fear of mishandling our opportunities. Perhaps several of the 52 ideas detailed on these pages will serve as basic tools to encourage and enable you to take the first steps and reach out with an open heart and loving arms.

As you contemplate reaching out to someone, turn to God, who promises to equip us for all good things. Then proceed with the assurance of God's promises to be with you "in the day of trouble." Touching the life of a person who is grieving gives you strength, confidence, and coping skills for other losses in life. With each experience you become more compassionate, confident, and understanding. Your potential for better understanding another person's pain and being a supporter increases.

Second Reminder: Three Actions

As you've read the ideas in this book, perhaps you've caught variations on three actions. Three *H* words, when grouped together, serve as a simple way to remember the three most important techniques you can put into practice.

Do: Hug them.

Say: "I'm so saddened by your loss. May I give you a hug?"

Give physical reassurance that you care. Extra hugs, hand-holding, and eye contact can be as important as anything you might say. It has been estimated that most of us need 11 hugs per day to flourish. At times of grief, we need more touch precisely because one key source of those hugs has been taken from us.

Do: Hang around.

Say: "I'll just be over here for a while."

Do: Hush.

Say: Nothing. Listen! Listen to "the story" again and again.

Say these three phrases three times fast.

Hug them, hang around, hush!

Hug them, _____ around, hush!

Hug them, _____ around, _____!

Commit them to memory:

_____ them, _____ around, _____!

We know that we have a gracious God in Jesus Christ. He suffered and died on the cross to give us the free gift of everlasting life. Yet He triumphed over the grave in His resurrection. Because of His death and resurrection, we have a certain hope of eternal life with Him. And because of this we can say and do things to show Christian sympathy to those who grieve.

Recommended Books

Barker, Peggy. *What Happened When Grandma Died.*
St. Louis: Concordia Publishing House, 1984.

Carter, Stephen. *The Master's Touch: Living with Grief.*
St. Louis: Concordia Publishing House, 1995.

Marxhausen, Joanne. *If I Should Die, If I Should Live.*
St. Louis: Concordia Publishing House, 1975.

Sims, Darcie D. *Why Are the Casseroles Always Tuna?*
Colorado Springs: Bereavement Publishing, 1990.

Strommen, Merton and Irene. *Five Cries of Grief.* San
Francisco: Harper Press, 1993.

Westberg, Granger E. *Good Grief.* Minneapolis:
Fortress Press, 1962.

Resources

The Compassionate Friends
  P. O. Box 3696
  Oak Brook, IL 60522
  (630) 990-0010
  www.compassionatefriends.org

Sudden Infant Death Syndrome Alliance
  1314 Bedford Ave., Suite 210
  Baltimore, MD 21208
  Landover, MD 20785
  (800) 221-SIDS
  www.sidsalliance.org

National Hospice and Palliative Care Organization
  17 Diagonal Road, Suite 625
  Alexandria, VA 22314
  (703) 243-5900
  www.nhpco.org